ALL AVILA
AND ITS PROVINCE

Text, photographs, design, lay-out and printing, entirely created by the technical department of EDITORIAL ESCUDO DE ORO, S.A.

Editorial Escudo de Oro, S.A.

Close-up of the stained-glass windows at the Saint John of the Cross Recreational Centre, an institution sponsored by the Caja General de Ahorros y Monte de Piedad de Avila *(Savings Bank).*

The famous Bulls of Guisando. ▷

KNIGHTLY AVILA

Avila is located on a hill at the foot of the Sierra del Guadarrama with the Paramera Range as a backdrop; it is irrigated by the waters of the river Adaja. At an altitude of 1,127 metres, it is the highest above sea-level of all the cities in Spain. Avila is perfectly walled. Miguel de Unamuno wrote: «one enters the city through doors, walking beneath stone lintels, just as one would enter a house (...) And when, within the walled enclosure, in the centre of the city, one comes across any of its squares, it seems to be positively expansive in its smallness. These peaceable sedate little squares that open out in the monastery area of the not merely old but eternal Castilian city!». Camilo José Cela, in turn, says that «of all the cities of Castile, Avila is possibly the most Castilian». It is also one of those with the oldest origins. The Celtiberian civilization was the first to leave its mark on the lands

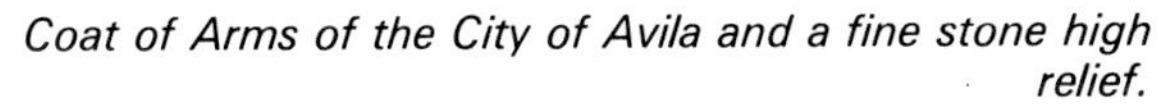

Coat of Arms of the City of Avila and a fine stone high relief.

Overall view of Avila and its walls.

of Avila, it has left us burial stones, sculptured groups of boars and above all, the famous Toros (Bulls) of Guisando.

The Romans subsequently settled the town and incorporated it into Lusitania naming it *Avela.* Avila bore several different names in ancient times: from *Obila,* as Ptolemy named it, to *Abela* as it is cited in the decrees of the council of Toledo; passing through *Abila* which is the name used by Saint Jerome and by Priscillian, and *Abula,* as it is mentioned in the historian Idacio's *«Chronicle».*

The episcopal see of Avila was founded towards the year 65 or 66, and presided over by San (Saint) Segundo, one of the Seven Apostolic Barons sent to Spain by Saint Peter, who was martyred in the town and succeeded by San Julio who thus became the second bishop of Avila. At the beginning of the 16th century a walnut casket was discovered in the church of San Sebastián — at present the hermitage of San Segundo — with, inside, human remains covered with priestly vestments, a mitre, a 15th century ring, a 14th century Gothic chalice and a stone carved with the inscription *«Sanctus Segundus».* Although there were in the tomb objects of a much later date than the death of San Segundo — which, however, in no way proves that the remains found are not those of the first Bishop of Avila — the public rejoicing of the citizens of Avila caused the ashes of the martyr to be considered genuine and he was consequently proclaimed patron saint of the city.

View of the whole of Avila at night.

San Vicente, Santa Sabina and Santa Cristeta, who were brothers and sisters, were also martyred in Avila, during the rule of the Roman emperor Diocletian.

The Visigoths settled Avila after the Romans and under their domination the town underwent a period that was rather grey in historical terms. The Visigoths left no important architectural monuments.

The Arabs conquered the town in the early 8th century, under the command of Tarik; they rased the Roman walls and rebuilt them solidly. In 742 Alfonso I «the Catholic» succeeded in taking possession of the town; it was reconquered by Abderraman I forty-three years later. Avila was controlled by Moslems and Christians in turn until Alfonso VI reconquered

Close-up of the shrine of Cuatro Postes.

San Vicente gate in the walls of Avila.

Toledo in 1085 and charged Raimundo of Burgundy with the repopulation and fortification of Avila. This was when the present city walls were built; they were finally finished in 1099.

The knightly period of Avila's history began shortly after. In 1105 Sancho Sánchez Zurraquín was leading a legion of knights from Avila against the Arabs in the area of Zaragoza when he went into battle with the shout, coined there and then, of «Avila, knights!». After the victory, the noble nickname began to be used: *«Knightly Avila».*

From this time on and for a long period which stretched to the last few years of the Middle Ages, Avila was the protagonist, directly or indirectly, of extraordinary historical events. Chivalry was almost always present, in one manner or another, in the unfolding of many of them. An example was the fantastic episode of 1109 when Jimena Blázquez, at the head of a motley army of women disguised as warriors, managed to defend Avila from siege by Arab troops when, at the same time, the knights of Avila were fighting against the Moslems far from the town. Another knightly episode was that of the sixty knights demanded as hostages by Alfonso I «the Warlike», whose troops were laying siege to Avila, in order to meet his stepson Alfonso in the town. According to the legend, the sixty knights of Avila were murdered and their heads cooked in oil. The place where the tragedy occurred is now known as «Las Hervencias» and the gate through which the unfortunate hostages

Close-up of the San Vicente Gate.

The fine Alcázar gate in the city walls.

left the town is called «Puerta de la Malaventura». The knightly continued overlapping the royal period after Alfonso VII conferred the title «Avila del Rey» on the city. As late as 1177 the knights of Avila won immense glory in the conquest of Cuenca and in 1246 in that of Jaén. Alfonso X «the Wise» granted the knights of Avila the right to always ride into battle in the vanguard.

An important event in the historical evolution of Avila was Juan II's decision in 1436 to impose the «Avila pot» — *«que face doce celemines»* as the legal and obligatory unit of volume in the whole of Castile.

Avila attained considerable importance in the 16th century as a result of having many flourishing industries, especially of textiles. Avila can curiously enough, also be considered in that century as the town «of saints and song», a felicitous expression of Queen Doña Juana's. On the 28th of March 1515 Teresa Sánchez de Cepeda Dávila y Ahumada, the celebrated authoress of *«Las Moradas»* was born in Avila. Together with Saint John of the Cross, also from Avila, she was to raise Spanish mystical poetry to the highest peaks. The whole city is full of Teresian traces and still impregnated with her poetic spirit. With the expulsion of the Moors in the early 17th century, Avila began to decline as an industrial centre. In successive centuries the city was to be transformed into a retiring, deeply loved urban nucleus with as its greatest charm the art which its fine monuments preserve.

The apse of the cathedral, popularly known as «cimorro».

Night-time view of the walls.

Several views of the ramparts of Avila.

THE CITY WALLS

It has been said that Avila is one of the best-walled cities in the world. It may be added that it is one of the most finely walled cities of all the Middle Ages. Avila would be architecturally unimaginable without the characteristic, unmistakable outline of its walls. They are a vitally necessary feature of the city. There is an implicit reference to the walls of Avila — the key word *«almena»* (battlement) — in these beautiful lines of Saint John of the Cross:

The wind from the battlements
when I spread her hair,
with her serene hand
wounding my neck,
suspended all my senses.

The walls are an artistic historical link of stone between the past and the present of Avila.
The building of the city walls of Avila was the first enterprise undertaken by Raimundo of Burgundy — also known as Count Don Ramón — by special order of Alfonso VI in order to fortify the Carpetanian cornice against Arab incursions. It is in fact the earliest monument of its class in Europe. The building work was begun at the end of the 11th century under the supervision of the «maestros de jometría» (the masters who controlled the joining of the stones in such buildings), the Roman Casandro Colonio and Florín de Pituenga, the Frank. Alvar García also intervened at a later date.
The foundations of the city walls were blessed by Bishop Don Pelayo of Oviedo, who had led the first expeditions to repopulate the town after its reconquest by Christian troops.
Avila's walls were constructed in nine years, from 1090 to 1099. It is impossible to state the exact

Curious close-up of the walls.

The ramparts with the river Adaja in the foreground.

A view of Puerta del Puente.

number of men who worked on the task but it seems, according to authoritative specialists in this field, to have varied between 1,900 and 3,000. Conquered Arabs were recruited to make up a large part of the labour force.

There can be no doubt but that the ramparts constitute a masterpiece of the military engineering of the period. The walls surrounded the city entirely and not only represented an impregnable bastion against any rising on the part of the Moslems, but have survived perfectly intact through the centuries and now form a monument of incalculable historical and artistic value. The ramparts have a perimeter of approximately a mile and a half. Their average height is 12 m., and the walls are up to 3 m. thick. There are 88 fortified towers of semicircular ground plan, 9 gates and 4 sally-ports, these last now walled up. «There are so many towers and they are so enormous», writes José María Salaverría, «that in the end they obsess us. We see them rise and protrude all over the place. They are everywhere, and are really the essential characters of the city and the only subject, the hero of the vista. They are, indeed, not mere conglomerations of granite, but people. People possessed of souls and characters that with changes of light and of time of day are transformed into a vague, refined sensibility. Tacit protagonists, lined up on the rampart, like a squad of soldiers tacitly distributed by the captain...». The city walls are made of stone-work and in some parts they boast an ornamental frieze of bricks at the top. Materials from the previous walls, Roman and Arab, were used in their construction, as were the remains of other buildings destroyed in Moslem attacks. Amongst the elements used in the construction of the Mediaeval walls one may remark various pre-Roman altar stones (which display mouldings and designs representing plants and fishes), fonts, inscriptions, numerous ashlars, empty stone moulds, stone tablets with Latin inscriptions and funeral steles showing primitive legends of heads of human beings. There are even authors who state that the present city ramparts contain walls originating from the ruins of an ancient Celtic settlement, a remote precursor of Avila.

Several views of the city walls and the river Adaja at their feet.

A close-up of the walls of Avila.

The city walls were built in the Romanesque style and one can also perceive some ornaments of Moorish influence in its architectural structure, such as lanceolate arches in certain inner doors of the brick turrets; and brick fretwork decorating the lower part of occasional barbicans. This fine massive monument was subsequently altered — especially during the 16th century — but none of the alterations detracted from its characteristic physical appearance.

The east flank of the walls, that is, the section stretching from Plaza de San Vicente to Plaza del Mercado Grande, is the oldest and the solidest. The most powerful bastions were raised here due to the particular disposition of the plain outside the city in this area, which facilitated the approach of enemy troops from that side.

Nevertheless, the most attractive view of the city walls is the north side, that is to say, the view to be had from the Mirador de Avila — a vantage-point located at the cross-roads of the Salamanca road and the one to Martiherrero, — from the *Monasterio de la Encarnación* or from the *Cuatro Postes*.

The most important gates are those of the Alcázar and of San Vicente, which are on the east side. That is also where the cathedral apse, with its «cimorro» three times paid homage to, joins the ramparts. In the same area is the Torreón del Homenaje, with two loopholes, which formed a part of the defences of the Alcázar. The aforementioned gates are made up of a pair of towers 20 m. high with a projection of 13 m., and 7 ½ m. thick; bridge, openings for dropping boiling oil etc., on assailants, and recesses in the flanks,

The city walls as an integral part of the landscape of Avila.

these last now blocked. The gates provided extraordinary possibilities for defence, combining the strength of the wooden doors and portcullis with the opportunity to set up cross-fire by firing from the two towers and from the bridge and machicolation.

The gate of San Vicente — and also the Alcázar gate — originally featured battlements of the same kind as the rest of the city wall. The present-day battlements of the San Vicente gate, arranged like a step-ladder, were built by Bernal de Mata in 1517, while those on the Alcázar gate are much more recent. This latter gate bears a stone tablet on the face of the bastion, referring to certain alterations carried out in the reign of Philip II.

The wicket-gate of the Mariscal, in the north face of the ramparts, is the only aperture which still retains its original structure. It acquired its name in the time of Juan II, because Don Alvaro Dávila, Major-General of Castile, had his residence nearby. It features a superb ogive arch.

Another interesting gate is that of the Carmen. It, too, is contained in the North face of the wall and there is a perceptible Moorish influence in its design. It is made of masonry and has square turrets; and was restored in the 14th century and also in later times. The *«Peso de la Harina»* gate, also called *«Puerta de los Leales»,* which is built of bossed masonry, is located in the east face of the city-walls between the San Vicente and Alcázar gates, in the place where the «Abbots' Wicket-Gate» used to be.

In the west side of the ramparts, opposite the river, there is the Arch of San Segundo, otherwise known as the *Arco del Puente.* Its towers are similar to those of the rest of the walls. The bossed granite part of this gate was rebuilt in the 15th century.

The Puerta de la Malaventura — through which the sixty knights alluded to in the legend of the *Hervencias* left the city — faces south and marks the beginning of the old Jewish Quarter.

The Santa Teresa gate, which was previously called *Puerta de Montenegro,* is of unquestionable interest.

A shot of the north part of the ramparts.

It is near the house in which this popular saint from Avila lived, and features square towers and machicolation.

The last gate is the *Puerta del Rastro,* which has in various periods also been called *«De Gil González Dávila», «de la Estrella»* and *«del Grajal».* The original square towers of this gate were rebuilt in the 16th century, they support an arch of impressive dimensions which constitutes a covered gallery. It features finely-wrought pillars and capitals that serve as corbels. A curious detail concerning the *Rastro* gate is that the opening of the entrance is not symetrically centred between the two towers.

Not only the *Torre del Homenaje* but also the bulwark tower were a part of the old Alcázar, a military fortress which must have played an important rôle in the Middle Ages. It seems that the Alcázar gate — nowadays one of the biggest in all the ramparts — gave access to a spacious parade ground inside which the warriors used to group together before making a sally and when preparing to defend their comrades who were fleeing from the enemy.

The Alcázar served as residence for Kings and powerful knights; but no longer subsists today. It was built in the 14th century, with large towers and Mudejar arches; and rebuilt using common rubblework in the 17th century. In the 18th-19th centuries, the Alcázar was used as a barracks.

Superb close-up of the Puerta de Santa Teresa.

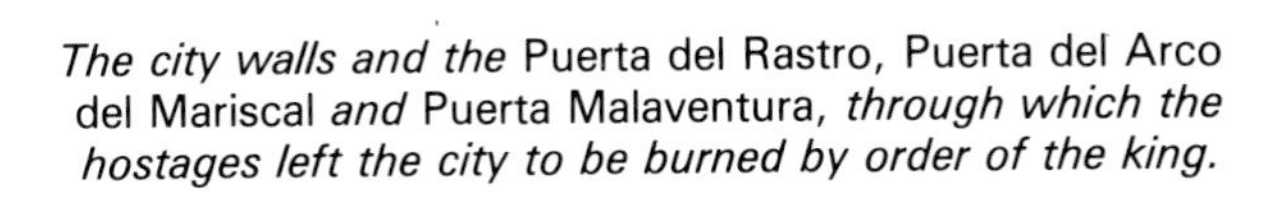

The city walls and the Puerta del Rastro, Puerta del Arco del Mariscal *and* Puerta Malaventura, *through which the hostages left the city to be burned by order of the king.*

A detail of the Cathedral's beautiful main door.

A detail of the North door of the cathedral church.

THE CATHEDRAL

From the outside it looks like a fortress; it was the first cathedral in Spain to be built to Gothic canons. Although there is no documentary evidence of the date when the building works began, we may be certain that they corresponded to a grant of money made, around 1135, by Alfonso VII. The documents state that the cathedral was rebuilt by his father, Raimundo of Burgundy, after some three hundred years of abandonment.
This reconstruction was apparently based upon a Romanesque cruciform ground-plan consisting of a transept and three apses, until Alfonso VIII appointed the master-builder Fruchel to direct the work. This architect died before the document which refers to Alfonso VII's grant for the cathedral was written in 1192. This architect was undoubtably French and knew well the building work which was being carried out on the Île de France. For this reason he no doubt had a low opinion of the sections of the Church that had already been built; it seems that he had the apses demolished so as to erect the large tower of the cathedral's new sanctuary, which he placed in the line of the city walls, thus considerably strengthening their defensive capacities. After Fruchel's death the architects who successively directed the works (their names are unknown) diverged from the ideas contained in his original plans; during the 13th century they built the sacrarium, the chapter-hall and the cloister. The cathedral church was practically completed in the 14th century, while Don Sancho Dávila was Bishop of Avila. Only slight architectural modifications were subsequently executed, of such a nature that they barely affected the original structure.
Two characteristics are harmoniously combined in Avila cathedral: the elements of a church and those of a fortress. Situated as it is next to the ramparts, it constitutes a part of their system of defence and can be considered not only a fortress but also the church

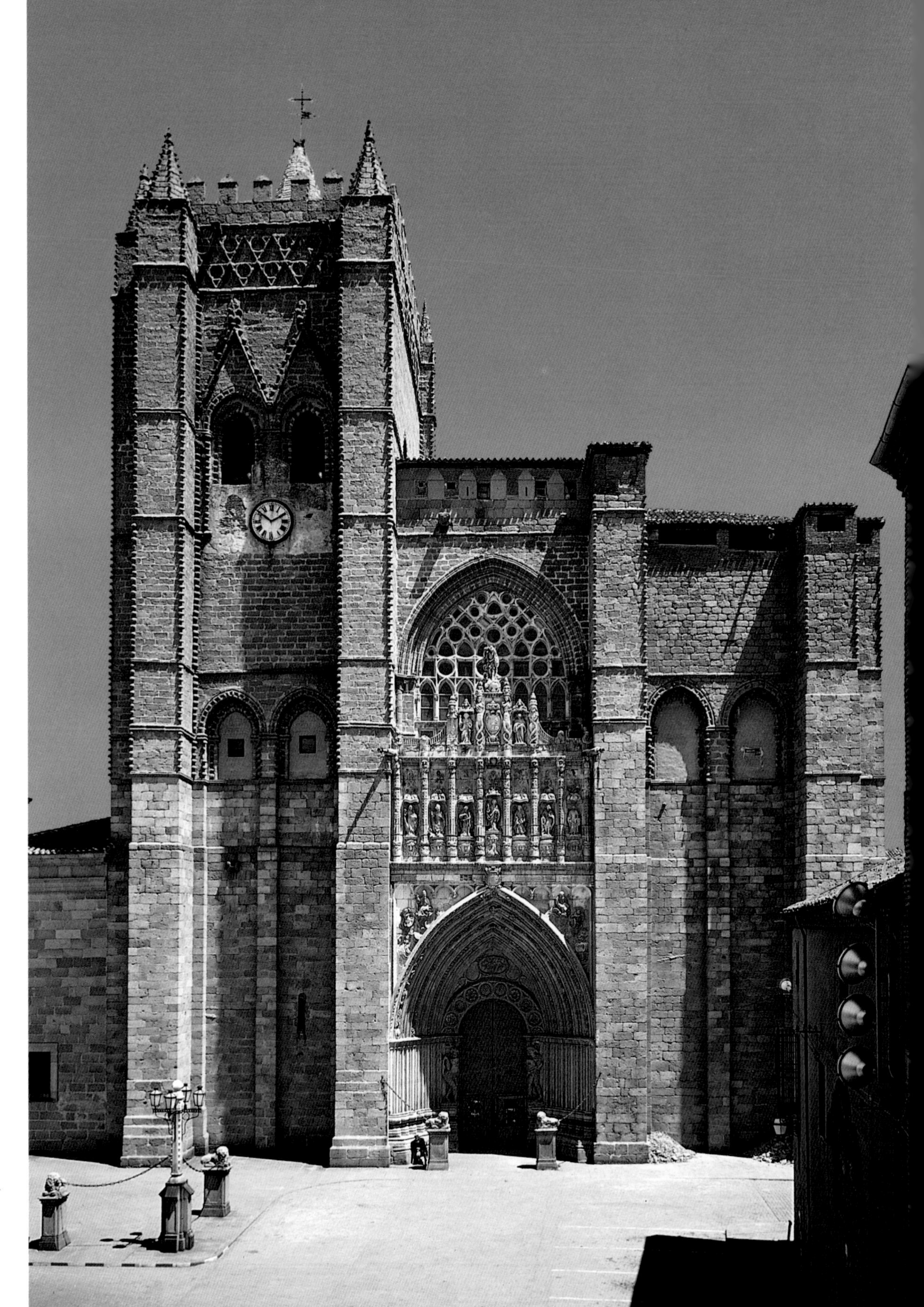

A fine close-up of the façade of Avila cathedral.

The nave of Avila cathedral.

The reredos in the retrochoir of the cathedral, a work by Juan Rodríguez and Lucas Giraldo.

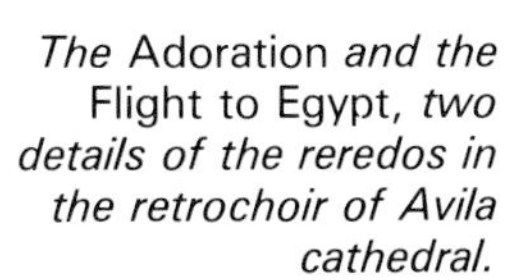

The Adoration *and the* Flight to Egypt, *two details of the reredos in the retrochoir of Avila cathedral.*

A splendid shot of the cathedral's superb choir-stalls.

(of its time) that best fulfils this function. The stone cathedral walls are very thick and surmounted by battlements. Both the massive tower in the east part of the cathedral — which has three sets of battlements, a gallery that is covered so as to make the most efficient use of the embrasures, and two walkways— and also the parade ground (where the liquids to be poured on to the enemy were boiled in enormous cauldrons) constitute martial structures that accentuate the fortress aspect of Avila cathedral. The same is true of the military gate which faces towards the west, and is surmounted by battlements, and of a second-line gate in the same wing.

Before the present roof was built, there were particularly fortress-like elements in the north and south wings too: for example, a double line of merlons with their respective paths behind. The ends of the cathedral transepts were built in such a way that they could play the part of flanking towers from which a cross-fire could be set up in combination with missiles discharged from the west towers.

Other typical characteristics of fortress design are similarly the cistern and two wells (one of which was directly supplied by a copious spring) which assured stocks of water in case of siege. The cistern, which is under the Velada chapel, is built of stone and comprises, in the main body, a rectangular ground-plan and lowered vault; also four radial galleries with barrel-vaults.

Until the 16th century, the Mayor of the Alcázar was

Close-up of the High-Altar reredos.

Close-up of the tomb of Don Alonso de Madrigal, «El Tostado», *Bishop of Avila.*

A detail of the tomb of «El Tostado», *by Vasco de Zarza.*

designated to make sure that the cathedral's defences were always in perfect condition. The Mayor's jurisdiction over the fortress-church was annulled in that century as a result of the continual frictions which had made the military and ecclesiastical authorities antagonists.

Sancho IV was proclaimed King of Castile in Avila cathedral in 1284; it was there, too, that Juan II's marriage to Doña María de Aragón took place in 1420. Another interesting episode of the cathedral's mediaeval history was when Don Alvaro de Luna, who was later to reach the position of Grand Master, was invested as knight of the Order of Santiago. The church — its chapter-halls, rather — was the chosen meeting-place of the anti-Enrique rebels in 1468 and also, in 1520, of the *Comuneros* of Castile who rose up against the centralism of Charles I of Spain, Charles V of Germany.

The appearance of Avila cathedral from the outside is extremely interesting. In the west front, which is the main façade, the outstanding sights are the north tower (completed in the first half of the 14th century), the unfinished south tower, and the doorway between the two, which was rebuilt in 1779 and is decorated with several statues originally from the previous door, carved by Juan Guas in the 15th century.

The statues of the sides of the doorway, which portray not the usual apostles but some fierce-looking men, catch the eye immediately. There is a small relief

The famous Monstrance by Juan de Arfe.

A close-up of the apse-aisle of the cathedral.

Close-up of the ceiling in the Chapter-Hall.

in the tympanum and others in the spandrels, these depict Saint Peter and Saint Paul and date from the 18th century. The upper part is decorated with a statue of the Saviour flanked by saints placed between columns, on ledges and under canopies. The door also features a pediment containing the arms of the cathedral in the centre and a number of statues at the sides, the whole surmounted by a statue of Saint

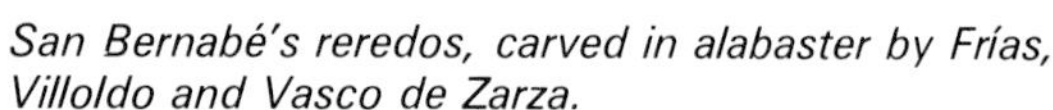

San Bernabé's reredos, carved in alabaster by Frías, Villoldo and Vasco de Zarza.

San Segundo's altar.

Michael the Archangel. Near the doorway there is a rose window which affords lighting to the nave.
The northern front displays a beautiful 13th century doorway, called the Apostles' door. This was previously under a porch in the main front; Juan Guas put it in its present position in the 15th century. The figures of the Apostles, statues of sober elegance, are placed on little columns and corbels. The Apostles bear serene expressions and have odd clothing and musical instruments.
The small canopies surrounding the figures of the Apostles are of five pointed archivolts, these display many richly carved groups of statues depicting symbolic scenes of the Last Judgement and the figures of saints and angels. There are three parts to the tympanum. The frieze in the lower part is decorated with various scenes from the life of Christ, among others the Last Supper; in the central part the Majesty of God, surrounded by angels, is outstanding; the upper part centres around the Coronation of the Virgin Mary. There are statues from an Annunciation — once installed in the doorway — in the pendentives of the archivolts. To the left of this façade a remnant of a Gothic wall is preserved, with two large 13th century pointed windows and a blocked 14th century rose window. The north front also offers the side part of the cathedral tower and the outside of the lofty nave displaying its windows and several fine flying buttresses.
The south front of the cathedral church is now hidden

A charming night-time view of Avila cathedral.

A triptych attributed to Fernando Gallego.

to a large extent by various buildings; the attraction of this façade centres on the novel relief of the Allegory which gave the Street of Life and Death its name, and on the cloister walls — bounded by this street and by *Calle de la Cruz,* — which sport fine cresting and a handsome pediment.
The façade that faces south is the least interesting. A pair of chained lions, sculptured at the end of the 18th. century, decorate the doorway. The beautiful gargoyles and the handsome cresting which tops the outside wall of the cloisters merit particular mention.
The interior of the cathedral has the shape of a Latin cross and is composed of a nave — 28 m. high — two aisles, a transept, an apse aisle, cloisters, a sacristy with its anteroom, a chapter-hall and a number of chapels built in different periods.
In architectural terms, the most interesting part is the sanctuary, composed of a double apse aisle with nine chapels, five of which — the ones in the centre — join the so-called «cimorro» or apse. Between the chapels there are substantial pillars of Gothic design with artistic capitals decorated with statues depicting human shapes, monsters and plants.
The most important feature of the internal precinct is the main chapel which is built in sandstone adorned with yellow, purple and red flecks and brought from the Valle Amblés; its style is transition Romanesque, with Mudejar additions in the mullioned windows.
The following are all worth particular mention: the magnificent principal reredos which is composed of 24 refined panels painted by Pedro Berruguete, Borgoña and Santa Cruz; the beautiful door to the

Sacrarium made of embossed silver and alabaster, fashioned by Vasco de la Zarza and García Crespo; and the excellent alabaster statue of Bishop Roelas. Saint Andrew's chapel is also of interest; it, and Saint Michael's as well, are situated in the old Catechumens' Vestibule, where one can also find the tombs of Deán Rui González, Esteban Domingo — chief of one of the factions which Avila was once divided into — and Blasco Muñoz, lord of Villafranca and Las Navas. Other outstanding items are: in San Ildefonso's chapel, the *«Altar de la Piedad»,* where the image of *«Nuestra Señora de la Caridad»* is worshipped; the two Gothic tombs in the Chapel of Saint John the Evangelist; Bishop Fray Hernando's Gothic tomb in Saint Nicholas' chapel; the reredos by Isidro Villoldo in the chapel of San Antolín; the Baroque altar, wall-paintings, bronze railings and the silver urn in which the remains of San Segundo are said to be preserved, all in the chapel bearing his name (Lope de Vega was its chaplain from 1626 to 1635); and the stained-glass windows and screens of the *Capilla del Cardenal.*

Still in the interior of the cathedral, the anteroom of the sacristy and the 14th century sacristy itself (also called San Bernabé's chapel), with splendid windows and a fine 16th century ivory crucifix, are similarly remarkable.

As well as the chapter-hall, the choir and the retrochoir, one must also mention the Cathedral Museum; there are pieces of considerable value in it, such as a large plateresque monstrance by Arfe; San Segundo's altar, a work by the 18th century silversmith García Crespo; a beautiful 16th century Gothic cross; an alabaster Ecce Homo carved by Vasco de la Zarza; a 12th century Gospel; and many others.

The Purification, *kept in the Cathedral Museum.*

The Annunciation, *kept in the Cathedral Museum.*

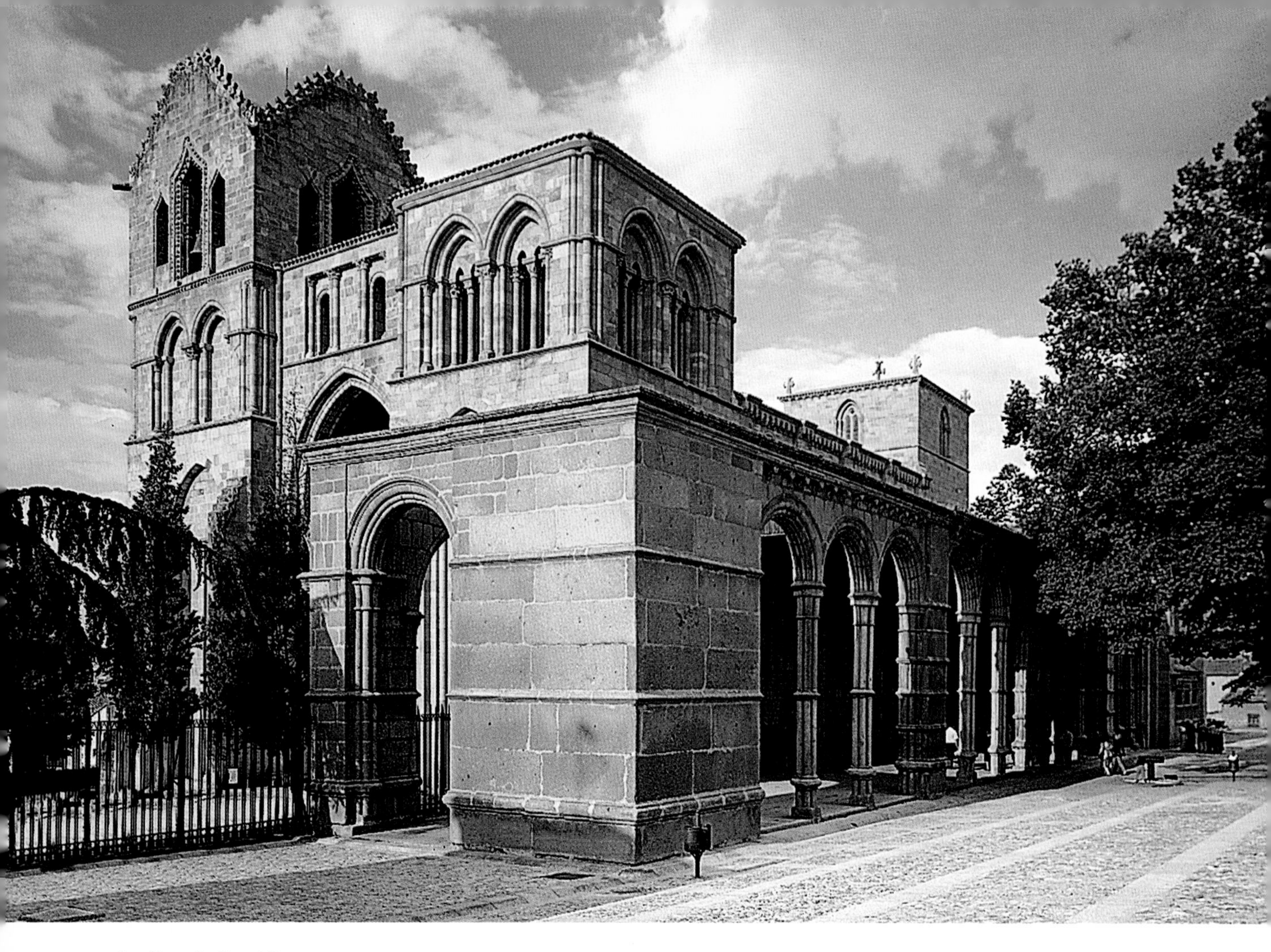

Basílica de San Vicente

SAN VICENTE

The foundation of the Basilica of San Vicente is connected with a curious legend involving three Christian siblings, Vicente, Cristeta and Sabina, who were cruelly martyred in Avila on the 27th October, 306.
According to the traditon, the lifeless bodies of the three martyrs were abandoned somewhere to the north of the town: their persecutors had flung them there to serve as sustenance for wild beasts. It seems that a snake took it upon itself to protect the bloody bodies of the three Christians; this is a quaint case since these reptiles always play detestable rôles in all kinds of legends. The miracle assumed proportions of popular fame when it was said that a wealthy Jew, accompanied by other members of the same faith, went to look at the bodies of Vicente, Cristeta and Sabina; when this Jew attempted to profane the corpses, the snake stopped him: he was deeply moved and exteriorized a wish to become a Christian convert, upon which the snake let him go. The converted Jew decided to raise a shrine to the three martyrs on that exact spot. This early chapel was the immediate precursor of the one that was built outside the walls of the old city in the 12th century, very near the cathedral. The foundations of the original chapel were apparently used in the building of the present-day basilica.
The building of the Basilica of San Vicente with the design that it has today started at the end of the 11th

Aerial view of the Basilica of San Vicente.

The doorway of the Basilica of San Vicente.

century when Raimundo of Burgundy began the task of repopulating and rebuilding the city of Avila. In 1109 the triple apse, the arms of the transept, the lower part of the nave and aisles, the crypt and the side doors had already been built. The whole edifice displayed the purest of Romanesque styles. Towards the year 1170, however, the style impressed on the building work at San Vicente became very similar to that displayed by the cathedral. This is why the specialists attribute the continuation of the Basilica of San Vicente to Fruchel.

There is another miracle connected with the Basilica of San Vicente around this time, the end of the 12th century. When San Pedro del Barco, the hermit, died in his native village, a controversy arose as to just where his remains should be buried. In order to clear up the question, the factions concerned placed the hermit's corpse on the back of a blind mule.

This creature set off towards Avila and entered the church of San Vicente, thereupon dropping dead on the floor of the transept. One of the mule's hooves

Part of the San Vicente Gardens.

The High-Altar in the Basílica de San Vicente.

Tomb of Vicente, Sabina and Cristeta, the Holy Martyrs.

made a carved print in the stone and San Pedro del Barco was buried in that precise spot.

The Kings San Fernando, Alfonso «the Wise», Sancho IV, Alfonso XI, Juan II and Queen Doña Isabel and Don Fernando ordered sundry alterations of San Vicente and the church acquired its present structure after the modifications directed by the architects Callejo and Repollés in the 19th and early 20th centuries.

The basilica has the shape of a Latin cross and comprises a nave, two aisles, dome, triforium, vestibule, a pair of towers and a crypt.

The front facing south is the most important, it features a lovely cornice crowning the upper part, with artistically very valuable corbels carved in high-relief; the curious rosettes are outstanding too. The doorway has superb statues.

The front orientated to the north is very lovely as well, although it displays less rich ornamentation than the south front.

In the east façade one can admire three fine Romanesque apses which boast magnificent carvings of dogs, the heads of symbolic animals, and leaves.

The west front is a fascinating work of art: its door-

A fine Romanesque statue of one of S Vincent's sisters, kept in the Basílica de San Vicente.

Statue of the Virgin of la Soterraña, *in San Vicente.*

The Adoration, *a detail of the tomb of the Holy Martyrs in San Vicente.*

way displays considerable ornamental richness. The archivolts are wonderfully decorated with lions, centaurs, sirens, birds of prey, griffins and other themes of masterly execution. The statues depicting the Apostles are also of unsurpassable quality.

The interior of the church is impressive for its majesty and its spaciousness. The most important aspects are: the triforium windows; the granite arches supporting the dome; the stone crucifix and statues of the Virgin Mary and Saint John located on the triumphal arch; the tombs of San Pedro del Barco and of the Israelite who founded the original church; the magnificent Romanesque screen which used to partition off the presbytery; the chapels of the apse, which are in Romanesque style; and the tomb of the martyrs Vicente, Cristeta and Sabina, a wonderful Romanesque piece dating from the 12th century.

The Soterraña, as the crypt is popularly known, consists of three chapels: they are reached via an unusual staircase of 29 steps with a vaulted roof.

«The Embrace», a 15th-century work by García del Barco, known as the Avila Maestro, kept in the Basílica de San Vicente.

Façade of the Real Monasterio de Santo Tomás.

Tomb of Prince Don Juan, the Reyes Católicos' *son.*

THE MONASTERY OF SANTO TOMAS

Saint Thomas' Monastery was founded by Doña María Dávila in fulfilment of the terms of her first husband Hernán Núñez de Arnalte's will. It stands on land which long ago belonged to the *Sancti-Spiritus* monastery and to Fernán González, canon of Avila, who was burned by the Inquisition along with his father, accused of being Judaists. The original monastery consisted only of what is now the sanatorium and the novices' cloister.

The building of Saint Thomas' Monastery began in

The High-Altar reredos of the Monasterio de Santo Tomás.

A view of the Museum of the Monastery of Santo Tomás.

1483 and took ten years. The costs were defrayed by Doña María Dávila, who contributed 1 ½ million maravedis, an annuity of 49,700 maravedis and 600 bushels of brown bread; and with the help of the *Reyes Católicos,* the so-called Catholic Queen and King, Isabella and Ferdinand, in the form of grants, privileges, exemptions and alms.

Torquemada, the famous Inquisitor, was present at the opening ceremony of the building works, and the Monastery — which was occupied by the Dominican Order from 1493 onwards — was the seat of the Court of the Inquisition. It was in this Court's chapel that the first *sambenitos,* or placards announcing the names of penitents and their penances, of all Castile were placed. The building served as summer residence for the *Reyes Católicos,* and was also a University for a long period commencing in 1504; the famous politician and writer Jovellanos studied there. After the monks were secularized in 1836, the monastery was bought by Don José Bachiller in 1844 and recovered by Isabel II in 1863; two years later she made it over to the bishopric, who returned it to the Dominican community in 1876.

The façade features a large Tudor arch over the doorway and the coat of arms of the *Reyes Católicos* surrounded by lions rampant, with the Yoke and Arrows carved on the upper part of the buttresses. The porch is decorated with limestone statues of the Saints of the Dominican Order of Predicants, Saint John the Baptist, Saint Catharine, the Virgin Mary and the Angel of the Annunciation. These works were carved by Diego de Siloé and Diego de la Cruz.

The interior of the church has the shape of a Latin cross and consists of a nave without aisles, with lateral chapels, chancel, choir loft, altars in the transepts and stylish Gothic fan vaulting. The following are particularly worth mentioning: the alabaster mausoleum of the *Reyes Católicos'* son — he died in Salamanca in 1497 at nineteen years of age — by Domenico Alessandro Fancelli, in the middle of the transept; the magnificent reredos by Pedro Berruguete in the main chapel; the alabaster tomb of the monastery's founder, Hernán Núñez Arnalte, in the *Capilla del Santo Niño;* the alabaster sarcophagus of Doña Juana Velázquez de la Torre and Don Juan Dávila, in Saint Catharine's chapel; the crucifix in front of which Santa Teresa had a long rapturous trance in the *Santo Cristo de las Angustias* chapel, where one can also see the consecrated host which was used by the murderers of the *Santo Niño de la Guardia;* the extraordinary Gothic choir-stalls; and the cloisters.

A curious litter shaped like a tower.

A Japanese vase in the Museo de Santo Tomás.

Overall view of the Hermitage of San Segundo.

The statue of San Segundo, by Juan de Juni.

The High-Altar of San Segundo. ▷

THE HERMITAGE OF SAN SEGUNDO

This hermitage is situated outside the ramparts of Avila, on the right bank of the river Adaja, in the place where, according to tradition, the house in which San Segundo lived used to be. The hermitage was previously known by the names of San Sebastián and Santa Lucía.

The church — in which the remains supposed to be those of San Segundo were discovered in 1519 — is Romanesque and dates from the 12th century. It is of modest proportions, comprising three apses, a belfry and a wooden roof. Part of the walls, the doorway and the apses date from the original church.

The interior of the hermitage is impressive for its simplicity; it is divided into a nave and two aisles, with unadorned columns and semicircular arches; these, like the small doorway which faces west, are 16th century.

The really important thing in this little church is the tomb of San Segundo, a work carved in alabaster by Juan de Juni in 1573. It is considered to be one of the best pieces by this famous artist. Popular devotion to San Segundo is as old as it is intense and his devotees still maintain the belief that if one places a handkerchief in San Segundo's tomb, he grants one's wish. By the side of San Segundo's tomb is Santa Barbada's, she was the young woman who changed into a man so to escape from the suit of a passionate gentleman, in the time of the Visigoth king Recesvinto. The maid attained this metamorphosis when, in the nearby hermitage of San Lorenzo, she begged God to deliver her from her own beauty in order not to fall into temptation and sin in the embraces of her love-struck persecutor.

The principal reredos is Baroque and made up of a number of painted panels depicting Saint James, Saint Anthony, Saint Michael, Saint Bartholomew, Saint Gregory, Saint Bernardine, Saint Peter and Saint Paul.

The façade of the Convento de Santa Teresa.

Convento de Nuestra Señora de Gracia.

On San Segundo's saint's day, a large number of the inhabitants of Avila flock to the hermitage so as to worship, on their knees, the city's patron saint.

NUESTRA SEÑORA DE GRACIA

The Augustine Convent of *Nuestra Señora de Gracia* was founded by Doña Mencía de San Agustín in 1509 and is situated in the outskirts, at the foot of the Alcázar tower, in the place where a rich Arab's mansion used to stand. A year after its foundation the nearby hermitage of *Santos Justo y Pastor* became the convent's church. Doña Ana, daughter of Don Juan de Austria, was imprisoned in the *Convento de Nuestra Señora de Gracia* for three years as a punishment for having a love affair with Gabriel de Espinosa, the famous pastrycook from Madrigal who passed himself off as King Don Sebastián of Portugal.

Santa Teresa, still known as Teresa de Ahumada, entered the Augustine College of the *Convento de Nuestra Señora de Gracia* as a pupil when she was 17. This was in 1531 and it seems that the future saint's father, Don Alonso, decided to confine her in order to prevent from developing the relationship which the young Teresa is said to have had with her cousin Pedro Alvarez Cimbrón. The legend referring to Santa Teresa states that, a few days before she entered the Convent and while the nuns were in the choir, a star appeared and alighted on Doña María de Briceño, who was later to be the personal tutor of the authoress of *«Las Moradas»*. Santa Teresa was in the Augustine College for a year and a half and the confessional box, communion rail and altar step which she used are still preserved.

The inside of the church has a nave without aisles and in the main chapel — founded by Don Pedro de Avila in 1551 — is displayed the magnificent Renaissance-style reredos which is attributed to Juan Rodríguez and Lucas Giraldo. The reredos is made up of twelve pictures depicting the Creator, the Assumption, a Virgin and Child, Saint Peter and Saint Paul and other religious themes.

A statue of Santa Teresa, the famous mystic from Avila.

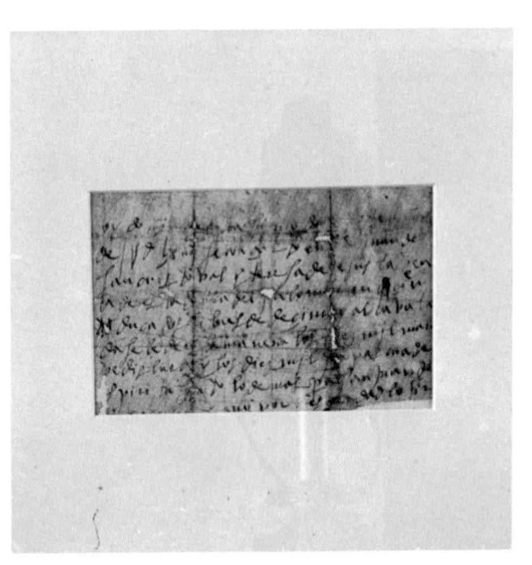

Four details of the beautiful stained-glass windows in the Discalced Carmelites' Church.

Two autographed letters, the rosary-reliquary and an espadrille which belonged to Santa Teresa, and the crucifix which presided over her cell.

The main front of the Monasterio de San José.

A detail of the statue of San José.

THE CONVENT OF SAN JOSE

This convent, which is also known as *de las Madres,* is the first one that Santa Teresa founded; it was formally opened on Saint Bartholomew's day in 1562. The church, in Herrerian style, was built later: the building work began under the direction of Francisco de Mora in 1607 and was finished three years later. Don Lorenzo de Cepeda — Santa Teresa's brother, Doña Guiomar de Ulloa and Bishop Don Alvaro de Mendoza all sponsored the enterprise. The interior has a single nave and six chapels, and the relics of Santa Teresa are the most important item.

The façade of the church of San Pedro.

The apse of the church of San Pedro.

Overall view of the Convento de la Encarnación.

THE CONVENT OF LA ENCARNACION

This convent was opened on the 4th April, 1515, the same day as Santa Teresa was baptised. The saint was to live in the *Convento de la Encarnación* as a nun for twenty-seven years, leaving in 1562 so as to found the Convent of San José. She returned to *La Encarnación* as prioress eleven years later and remained there for three years more. Saint John of the Cross, San Francisco de Borja and San Pedro de Alcántara visited her at the Convent many times.
The façade of *La Encarnación* is conserved just as it was in Santa Teresa's time, except for the bell-gable on the tower, which was built in 1715 by Fray Julián Cano, a barefoot carmelite and Bishop of Avila, whose coat of arms figures between the bays of the belfry. The doorway, which is Avilan Renaissance-style, consists of a round arch with large voussoirs. The coats of arms on the embrasure are of Don Nuño González del Aguila, who financed the alterations made to the convent in 1526. The ensemble of the façade, built of granite blocks, is surmounted by a wooden relief depicting the mystery of the Incarnation *(La Encarnación).*
The interior of the church was altered in the first half of the 18th century and has a Latin cross ground-plan with a single nave, barrel vaults and a dome with pendentives and a lantern. The greater part of the altars and décor are Baroque, but the basic structure, the screens of the two choirs, the communion-rail of

the lower choir and the doors of the inner recess date from Santa Teresa's time.

The altar dedicated to Saint John of the Cross has a statue of the great mystic and a small one of Santa Teresa. In Saint Anne's chapel there is a painting of Teresa, the Saint of Avila; and, to the left of the transept, is the 'Capilla de la Transverberación,' built on the site of one of S Teresa's cells.

In the part of the Convent closed to outsiders there is a parlour in which Santa Teresa's office used to be installed and another which was her cell as a nun. The Prioress's seat in the lower choir where the Saint sat is kept as a Teresian relic.

In the closed part there are also several relics of the Saint, among them a crucifix which she took with her on her travels, a fragment of her habit, a towel, a small pitcher, a jug, a deed of endowment with her signature and several letters. A drawing by Saint John of the Cross is also preserved.

The legend has it that it was in a parlour on the ground floor that the levitation of Santa Teresa and Saint John of the Cross occurred.

The interior of the church at the Convento de la Encarnación.

Plaza de Santa Teresa: Palace of Blasco Núñez Vela and the Convent of La Santa.

THE NUÑEZ VELAS' PALACE

This palace now houses the installations of the court buildings. The façade of this Plateresque building is one of the most beautiful of all the civil architecture in Avila. The palace, which is situated in the evocative Plaza de La Santa, was built by Blasco Núñez de Vela, alderman of the city and Viceroy of Peru, in the middle of the 16th century, as can be gathered from the letter he sent to the town council of Avila on 4th April, 1542: «You know already of the house I am making in this city, the same will be an ornament for it». Blasco Núñez Vela was descended from Don Pedro Núñez de la Fuente Alnexir, the intrepid knight who became famous for his heroic exploit when he took the child Alfonso VIII to Avila hidden under his cape so that he should not become entangled in the cruel fratricidal struggle in which the Castros faction was confronting the Laras.

Núñez Vela later died in the Battle of Iñaquitos, fighting extraordinarily bravely against the rebels led by Gonzalo de Pizarro. Don Antonio de Cepeda, Santa Teresa's brother, lost his life in this same battle, and another relative of the noble family, Don Rodrigo, eldest son of Doña Beatriz de Ahumada, was seriously injured.

The main doorway of the palace's splendid Plateresque façade is outstanding, it has a round arch and elegant, elongated voussoirs with two handsome columns topped by the coats of arms of Blasco Núñez Vela. The courtyard is also very interesting, with its galleries of Doric columns and refined staircase.

Coats of arms of Blasco Núñez Vela.

The patio of the Palacio de Blasco Núñez Vela.

Coat of Arms on the Palacio de los Dávila.

An angle of the patio of the Palacio de los Dávila.

THE DAVILAS' PALACE

It is located in the Plaza de Pedro Dávila and is one of the buildings most representative of mediaeval Avila's knightly spirit. This nobleman's mansion was built in the 13th century and restored in the following 200 years by the descendants of Esteban Domingo, the founder of the powerful Dávila family.
In fact, it consists of four inter-connecting buildings which extend from the Episcopal Palace towards the *Puerta del Rastro.*

The oldest house is built onto the ramparts and features a beautiful 13th century ogive porch with cylindrical Romanesque mouldings and fine carvings of plants; the thirteen roundels distinctive of the Dávilas' coat of arms are displayed on the capitals of the second floor.
Another building features a 14th century straight arch with corbels depicting heads, carved sphinxes and, on the second floor, a mullioned coat of arms.
The façade of Navamorcuende displays a doorway with elegant wedge-pieces and the Dávila family arms

Three views of the Palacio de los Dávila.

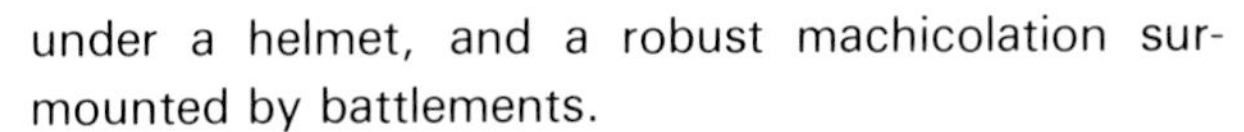

under a helmet, and a robust machicolation surmounted by battlements.

Another façade, called «of the Navas», features on its face a series of high reliefs recounting the thirteen roundels victory, these symbolise the thirteen villages whose standard Hernán Pérez Dávila seized from the Moors in the attack on Ronda.

Other interesting details are a fine Mudejar panelled ceiling and the Celtiberian boars in the courtyard.

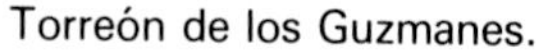

Torreón de los Guzmanes.

Seat of the Provincial Government.

THE CITY

Unamuno writes: «Contemplating Avila one can understand how and whence Santa Teresa got the idea of her images of the interior castle, of the dwellings and of the diamond. For Avila is a granite diamond gilded by the suns of centuries and by centuries of suns. How many?» Many, certainly. At the least the long Middle Ages which left the varied mark of their knightly and religious spirit on the city. The whole of Avila is impregnated with mediaeval traces, starting, of course, with the incomparable city walls. The most complete views of the city's singular configuration are, perhaps, to be had from the Salamanca road. In particular, a splendid panorama of Avila, presented to the visitor bounded by the mediaeval ring of the ramparts, may be viewed from the distinctive *Cuatro Postes,* in the centre of which there is a cross; it is indeed a place where processions are held and where people often go to photograph angles of Avila.

The city walls impress not only by their monumental dimensions and robust martial appearance, which has been perfectly conserved over the centuries, but also because they fit harmoniously into the landscape, forming a compelling link between the city and the surrounding countryside. One would almost say that the walls had sprung up spontaneously from the ground, that they had been where they are since the dawn of time. The sun settles on their towers and

The monument to Saint John of the Cross.

Verses from the «Cantico Espiritual» *on the monument to the mystic.*

battlements like an old acquaintance gilding their ridges and arousing in the onlooker the free flight of his imagination and fantasy. A stroll around the ramparts represents a real feast for the eyes and is also the best way to get an idea of Avila's personality as a city. Such a walk furthermore permits one to enjoy views of extraordinary beauty and to approach with one's sight and spirit such fascinating corners and monuments of Avila as *La Encarnación, el Pradillo,* the ruins of San Francisco, San Andrés, the curious *Ajates* quarter, the hermitages of San Martín, San Segundo and *Nuestra Señora de la Cabeza,* the river Adaja, the Romanesque bridge, the San Nicolás quarter, the valley of Amblés and the bluish backbone of the mountains. A whole film of landscapes in full colour, composed of varied forms that are always in harmony with the whole...

The beautiful *Plaza de Santa Teresa* is one of the most suitable parts of Avila from whence to begin one's discovery of the city. From there one can reach the most attractive corners of the walled city by taking a leisurely walk down any of the neighbouring streets, with one's eyes always open for astonishing sights.

The *Paseo de San Roque,* which is flanked by long benches and faces south, is one of the parts of the city with most character. This used to be one of the best vantage-points from which to survey the city, but the development of one side now blocks the view of the landscape made up by the *Valle Amblés,* the *Convento de Santo Tomás* and the greyish background of the mountains.

The Paseo del Rastro is an excellent viewpoint for looking south, from it one may see a charming vista of the San Nicolás and Santiago quarters and the river Adaja. The *Paseo* finishes towards the west in a beautiful tree-shaded garden with a fountain, and from this vantage-point one can look down on the roads leading to the city which on Fridays, market day in Avila, fill up with country people who come to sell their produce.

Aerial view of Plaza de Santa Teresa.

The *Parque de San Antonio,* which is on the left of the railway station, is another pleasant corner of the city. It is a fine garden with wide paths lined with trees and several ornamental fountains.

The *Jardín del Dos de Mayo* is also worth a visit, it is near the *Parque de San Antonio* and backs onto the wall of the *Convento de Santa Ana's* kitchen-garden. The bandstand on which the municipal band of Avila gives its concerts stands here.

There is a particularly enjoyable walk to be had from San Vicente to the *Cuatro Postes:* after leaving the gateway one continues to the Adaja towards the north and west of the walls and crosses the bridge.

Another evocative excursion is to the *Hervencias,* walking along the Villacastín road. The legend relates that the heads of the sixty knights of Avila demanded as hostages by Alfonso VII's stepfather were boiled here, next to a fountain among rocks and pastures.

The Teresian itineraries are fundamental and absolutely necessary in Avila. The whole city is marked with traces of the Saint and monuments evoking her steps occur here and there over the length and breadth of the city. The key spot in this sense is the *Convento de Santa Teresa,* or simply *de la Santa,* as it is popularly known in Avila. It occupies the same place as did the much-travelled saint's father's house. The building dates from the 17th century and has a Baroque front divided into three sections. A magnificently carved statue of Santa Teresa by Gregorio Fernández is kept inside the church, in the self-same room where Teresa de Cepeda y Ahumada was born. The garden of the old house is also preserved and the following Teresian relics are venerated in a small room: a finger from her right hand, the staff she used on her journeys, her rosary, the sole of one of her sandals and some autographical letters.

Other Teresian landmarks include the church of San Juan, in the centre of the city, where the saint was

A view of the historical Calle de la Muerte y la Vida.

The Hermitage of Cristo de la Luz *and a cross.*

baptised in the font on the 4th April, 1515; the convents of *La Encarnación,* San José and *Nuestra Señora de Gracia;* the Teresian Library set up in the *Casa de Cultura;* and the *Casa de los Guillamas,* where Santa Teresa lived in the period when she was planning her reform. Many other monuments enrich the city, among them the one erected in memory of Saint John of the Cross, the sublime poet from Avila, author of *«Cántico Espiritual».*

Magnificent close-up of Plaza de Calvo Sotelo in the city centre.

Belltower of the Chapel of Mosén Rubí.

Mansion of Los Polentinos.

Church of San Esteban.

The façade of Avila Town Hall.

Main front of the Palacio de los Valderrábanos.

The patio of the Palacio de los Bracamonte.

The façade of the Palacio de los Deanes.

THE VALDERRABANOS' PALACE

This palace is situated opposite the cathedral. It was built in the 15th century and of its original fabric it preserves an interesting Gothic doorway — with lintel and decorated with carved corbels, and the arms granted to Gonzalo Dávila for his brave conduct in the capture of Gibraltar in 1462 — and several fine windows in the upper part of the building.
The palace is at present a hotel.

THE BRACAMONTES' PALACE

This palace stands next to the Mariscal gate and belonged to Don Alvaro Dávila, Major-General of Castile, later becoming the property of the Count of Parcent and the Baron of Andilla. It seems that the palace was built in the 15th century, when Don Alvaro Dávila was lord of Bracamonte.
The most interesting part of the palace now is perhaps its beautiful courtyard which displays graceful escutcheoned pillars.

THE PALACE OF LOS DEANES

This is a Renaissance building which nowadays houses the galleries of the Art Museum of the Province. It lies in the *Plaza de Nalvillos* and was built in the mid-16th century.
The main front is built of masonry and composed of two floors, with five balconies and four low windows. It is elegantly decorated with two sets of pillars and capitals with corbels. The lower part of the upper floor displays pilgrims' scallop-shells and coats of arms with the cathedral chapter's arms. The Baroque cresting is very interesting; a sun-dial appears in the Baroque pediment. The rococo iron-work on the balconies, several grilles with Gothic influence, the courtyard and its two cloisters are also of interest.

Façade of the old Casa de la Misericordia.

THE HOUSE OF EL CABALLO

This building was an alms house in ancient times, and also the residence of Manso, the prebendary. The *Casa del Caballo* is in the *Calle de San Segundo,* near the cathedral. Of the old building, only the 16th century doorway remains: it is rectangular and contained between columns crowned with a frieze and torch-holders. Above the lintel there is a niche with a high relief depicting Saint Martin on horseback, sharing his cape with a beggar. Under the niche one may read an inscription which is as follows: *«Domus misericordie.* — This house was founded and endowed by Señor Rodrigo Manso, being prebendary of the church of Avila, for the poor of this city and to serve God».

The patio of the Casa de Paz.

OTHER PALACES

Avila is a city abounding in noblemen's mansions. One of the most important is the *Torreón de los Guzmanes,* which is in the *Plaza de Cepeda* and used to belong to the Oñate family and to the Countess of Crecente — it is now the property of the *Diputación Provincial;* the building was constructed in the 16th century within the characteristics of the transition from Gothic to Renaissance architecture. Others are the *Mansión de los Polentinos* in *Calle de Vallespín,* housing the *Academia de Intendencia;* the *Palacio de Henao* — now the «Raimundo de Borgoña» *Parador* (luxury State hotel) — in *Calle de los Caños;* the 16th century *Palacio del Marqués de Bermudo* in *Calle*

The statue of Nuestra Señora de Sonsoles.

The shrine of Nuestra Señora de Sonsoles.

Blasco Jimeno; the ***Palacio de los Villaviciosa y Sofraga,*** next to the San Vicente gate; the ***Palacio de los Aguila; Torre Arias;*** and the ***Casa de Paz,*** seat of the Chamber of Commerce.

THE HERMITAGE OF SONSOLES

This hermitage is situated on a hillock to the south of the city and surrounded by a copse. The Virgin of Sonsoles is the object of considerable popular devotion on the part of the people of Avila, especially the country people of the *Valle Amblés,* who have given her the nickname «La Divina Serrana». When there is a prolonged drought, the statue inside the Hermitage is taken in procession to the city.
The worship of the Virgin of Sonsoles is very ancient. According to popular legend, the statue of her was found by chance by the members of the cortège who were transferring San Zoilo's body from Córdoba to Carrión, towards the end of the 11th century, although there is another tradition to the effect that it appeared to a shepherd at an unknown date.
The Hermitage was rebuilt in 1480 and enlarged almost a century later. The church is structurally simple, with two buttresses and two doorways. The door of the main front has a round arch, medallions and carved suns; and the one facing south bears six suns circumscribed by a laurel crown. The church is situated on a plot of land with some fountains and the houses of the priest and the sanctuary-caretakers amid thick trees, the whole bounded by iron railings. This precinct is entered through a large, finely-designed doorway, with noble coats of arms, and two suns on the keystone of the arch.

Inside the church are a nave and two aisles with 16th century arches and columns and Baroque plastework vaults. With regard to the interior of the church, one should mention the Renaissance high-altar with the statue of the Virgin of Sonsoles in the centre and the shrine to the Virgin, which displays 15th and 16th century azulejos.
The pilgrimages of the«Little Offering» and the «Big Offering» are held at the shrine every year.

Monument to St. Teresa, which stands on the foundations of her home.

Altar in the parish church of Gotarrendura.

ST. TERESA OF JESUS

Head north out of the city of Avila and follow the left bank of the Adaja River and you will come to the town of Gotarrendura, which lies at the start of the wide plain of La Moraña.

This town is closely linked to the life of St. Teresa and particularly to her childhood. Her parents owned a large estate of land and livestock, which they had inherited from Doña Teresa de las Cuevas, the saint's maternal grandmother.

The inhabitants of the village, who then numbered ninety-five, were witness to the important events in St. Teresa's family. Her parents, Don Alonso Sánchez and Doña Beatriz de Ahumada, married in the autumn of 1509: the day was memorable for the whole village. The family spent many a long season here, for the harvest in summer and to escape the cold of Avila in the winter. Everybody, especially Don Alonso, loved this relaxing place.

In 1528 Doña Beatriz fell ill and died, and her body was taken to Avila.

Over the years, almost all of St. Teresa's brothers were to go to America and the estate was to be sold. The only thing now remaining from the Cepeda Ahumada country home is the base of a dovecote. According to traditional story, the stone from the house was used to build the existing parish church. St. Teresa was to call her convents «Palomaricos» after the «palomar» (dovecote) of her childhood home, where, in all simplicity and humility, glory is given to God.

FUNDACIONES DE LA MADRE TERESA
1562 ~ 1582
Orduña
Aguilar de Campoo
Pamplona
Palencia
Burgos
Valladolid
Soria
Zamora
Medina del Campo
Segovia
Salamanca
Avila
Pastrana
C. Rodrigo
Arenas de San Pedro
Madrid
Valencia
Alba de Tormes
Villanueva de la Jara
Torrijos
Toledo
Lisboa
Evora
Daimiel
Malagón
C. Real
Caravaca
Sevilla
Beas
Granada
MAR MEDITERRANEO

GASTRONOMY IN AVILA

The cuisine of Avila, with its mediaeval lineage, is generally a no-nonsense affair. It is a simple and basic approach to cooking, without the slightest suspicion of tricks or padding. There are various dishes which should be mentioned as outstanding. The first is the roast sucking pig, especially from Arévalo; but every bit as good are the roast lamb, fried trout — from the Alberche or Tormes rivers — the stewed partridge or the kid hot-pot. Avilan veal, the *chorizo* (salami) and cured ham from Navalperal and La Cañada, crayfish from the Adaja and Voltoya rivers and the French beans of El Barco de Avila are all justly famous too.
As for desserts, there is a wide and excellent choice: the exquisite «yemas de Santa Teresa», fruit from the banks of the Corneja and Tiétar rivers, peaches from Burgohondo, «albillo» grapes from Cebreros, water-melons from Lanzahita, the cherries of El Arenal, the apples of El Barco or pears from Villafranca.
There is also an excellent wine of considerable strength in the Avila region: it is from Cebreros and cannot be bettered as an accompaniment for roasts.

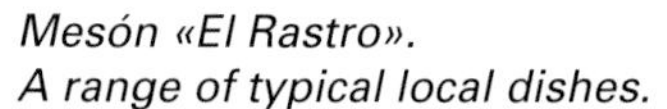

Mesón «El Rastro».
A range of typical local dishes.

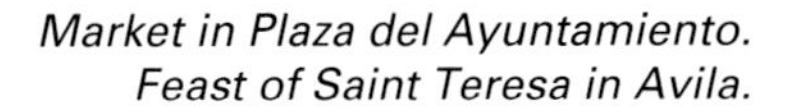

Market in Plaza del Ayuntamiento.
Feast of Saint Teresa in Avila.

FOLKLORE

The old ballads have a deep influence on the people of the province of Avila, as is general in all Castile; particularly in the *Valle de Amblés,* where some ancient songs survive. As for the dances, the most typical ones are the *rondón* (roundelay), the *jota serrana* and the *seguidillas.*

The typical masculine costume consists of tight short breeches, white shirt, dark-coloured jacket, woollen leggings or stockings and espadrilles or black shoes. The men generally have a wide-brimmed felt hat, worn somewhat twisted. The women wear mantles of coloured flannel, bodices of dark-coloured material, shawls with festoons, colourful skirts and straw hats adorned with ribbons, flowers and fragments of mirrors. Among the different variations on the traditional costumes distinctive of Avila province, those from Guisando and Candeleda are outstanding for their beauty.

The most important *fiestas* are those held in Avila from the 7th to the 15th of October, in honour of Santa Teresa; and the pilgrimages on the first Sunday of October — «Little Offering» — and on the second — «Big Offering» — to the *Santuario de Sonsoles.*

This atmospheric crossroad with three stone crosses is on the outskirts of Avila.

SIERRA DE GREDOS

This range of mountains as a whole constitutes an impressive example of the majestic beauty that Nature sometimes provides. The *sierra* played a very important rôle in history, as the front line of Castile's natural defences.

It forms part of the «Carpetovetónica» mountain range and constitutes the dividing-line between Old Castile and New Castile.

The north end of the Gredos massif is in the valleys of the rivers Alberche and Tormes, and its southern extreme is on the river Tiétar. The mountain range is remarkable for its strange, diverse beauty and it is, for the tourist, one of the most fascinating areas of the Iberian peninsula.

The landscape of Gredos joins the *meseta* (plateau) to the north and forms a singularly attractive stretch of countryside there, while to the south the *sierra* becomes wilder and wilder until it forms a colossal natural wall with New Castile.

Gredos is located in the middle of the central *cordillera* and extends from east to west, separating the valleys of the rivers Tajo and Duero. The part that is in the province of Avila makes up the catchment area of the Tiétar river, and shelters the beautiful Tiétar valley to the south.

The Central Massif of Gredos stretches from the *Puerto de Tornavacas* to *Puerto del Pico,* on the road leading from Avila to Arenas de San Pedro. The East Massif comprehends the area from *Puerto del Pico* to the river Alberche, which separates Gredos from the

Overall view of the Parador Nacional de Gredos.

Sierra de Malagón and the *Sierra de Guadarrama.* Lastly, the West Massif stretches from the *Puerto de Tornavacas,* on the road from Avila to Plasencia, to the *Puerto de Béjar,* and is interrupted on the west by the valley of the river Alagón.

The Central Massif, an area also called the «Andalusia of Avila» is particularly interesting. It is reached via the *Puerto del Pico* using the Avila — Arenas de San Pedro road. The majestic beauty of this area can hardly be described: you have to have the unique Gredos landscape before your eyes to be able to appreciate its strange, fascinating grandeur. The marvellous *Laguna de Gredos,* of glacial origin, may be admired in the locality named the Gredos stone cirque, or *Plaza del Moro Almanzor.* This lake is 2,000 m. above sea-level and surrounded by sheer walls of rock; the water is very deep and of an intense blue colour. The Hispanic mountain goat inhabits this area, giving a vivacious and exotic touch to the mountainous Gredos landscape.

Other very attractive places are *el Casquerazo, Los Hermanitos de Gredos, Hoya de Antón* and the other streams which debouch into the *Laguna de Gredos;* and the proud summits surrounding it: *El Cuchillar de las Navajas, la Portilla de los Machos* and *el Morezón.*

The *Parador Nacional* (first-class state hotel) *de Gredos* is in this mountainous part of the province of Avila and surrounded by incomparable landscapes: there are wide and beautiful vistas to be enjoyed from its installations. The *Coto Nacional de Gredos* nature reserve, habitat of ibex and other species, is not far from the *Parador.*

An overall view of Arenas de San Pedro.

ARENAS DE SAN PEDRO

This fine and sizable town in the province of Avila is located in a depression in the foothills of the *Sierra de Gredos,* surrounded by pinewoods in a landscape framed by marvellous vistas of mountains. Arenas de San Pedro is 524 m. above sea-level. Its fascinating personality as a town is underlined by its being the capital of the so-called «Andalusia of Avila».
Arenas de San Pedro is the centre of a vast district and the starting-point for outings to the Central Massif of Gredos.
One of the greatest attractions of the town — together with its curious urban structure and the delightful landscape which surrounds it — is, no doubt, the temperate climate which is in marked contrast to the presence nearby of the perpetual snow of the *Sierra.*
As if all this were not sufficient, Arenas de San Pedro offers the visitor a rich variety of monuments, the inheritance of a brilliant historical past. Apart from the 15th century Castle-Palace, which deserves a separate paragraph, the most noteworthy of its more important monuments are the Palace of Prince Don Luis de Borbón, Carlos III's brother, and the Monastery of San Andrés del Monte which was founded by San Pedro de Alcántara, who is buried there, with its octagonal chapel designed by Ventura Rodríguez and its important reredos by Gutiérrez. The monastery is now the home of the Franciscan missionaries of the Orient.
The church of the Assumption, with its lofty clocktower and refined reredos, should also be men-

The Plaza del Condestable Dávalos *in Arenas de San Pedro.*

tioned, as should the Roman bridges over the rivers Arenas and Pelayos.

The *Cueva del Aguila,* and other caves, were discovered recently in the environs of Arenas de San Pedro. Inside them one's attention is forcefully drawn to the stalactites and stalagmites which sketch fantastic natural shapes.

The atmospheric old castle of Arenas de San Pedro stands not far from a Roman bridge which spans a babbling brook that is always topped with foam. The widow of Don Alvaro de Luna lived in this castle, which is why it is called the Castle of the Sad Countess. The illustrious lady once wrote to King Juan II of Castile and started her letter in this manner: «I, the sad countess, Doña Juana Pimentel, lady of Montalbán, widow of Don Alvaro de Luna; and your cousin...»

Don Alvaro de Luna had been Lord High Constable of Castile. Juan Grande Martín writes: «He was genuinely loved by his first wife, Doña Elvira Portocarrero; other women hated him because they had loved him, and indeed they continued to love him, dreaming as they read his rondels. The barons envied the elegance of his person, his talent, his wit for expressing difficult philosophical concepts transformed into gallantries when literary contests were being judged; they also envied him his daring and his corteous valour whenever a lance was broken, in jest or seriously.»

But Don Alvaro de Luna's destiny was suddenly to turn adverse and finally became tragic.

The monument to San Pedro de Alcántara.

It seems that Isabel of Portugal, Juan II's second wife, was jealous of the power that Don Alvaro de Luna had attained in the court and influenced her husband to have the Lord High Constable of Castile imprisoned. He was later condemned to death and his possessions confiscated. His widow, Doña Juana de Pimentel, accepted the exchange that Juan II proposed to her — the castle of Escalona for the lordship of Arenas de San Pedro — and from then on she lived shut up in the town's castle, given up to the memory of her beloved late husband.

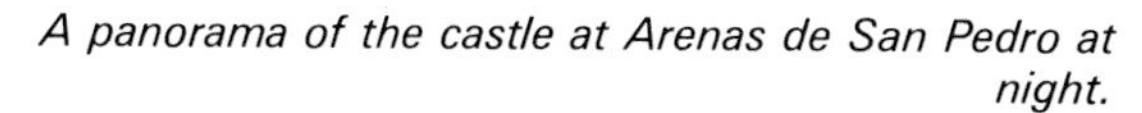

A panorama of the castle at Arenas de San Pedro at night.

Part of Arenas de San Pedro.

The church tower at Arenas de San Pedro.

The castle at Arenas de San Pedro is an extensive building with a square ground-plan, round towers on the four corners and square turrets to defend half of each side wall. The walls of the noble building, which is a National Monument, are now covered with ivy and moss; this helps to give its appearance a compellingly evocative and poetical touch, very much in harmony with its history.

The inside of the castle was apparently in perfect harmony with its architecture. Grande Martín, a historian who specialises in aspects of Avila, says «The rooms of the castle were distributed over two floors, on the south and west, and extended from the south-east corner to the Homage Tower, with the entrance on the first floor via a corridor with vaulting and ogive arches. The rest was the parade ground, with the stables and servants' and soldiers' rooms on the ground floor, the chapel, hall, rooms for guests, travellers and pilgrims... placed even in the turrets, depending on the standing of their functions. Dungeons in the lower part of the Homage Tower; ladies' drawing-room exclusively for Doña Juana Pimentel during her beloved husband's prolonged absences at the court. This drawing-room in the Homage Tower was even a chapel for Doña Juana Pimentel, living as in a nunnery when the Lord High Constable was away. (...) And she lacked nor a clavichord, a harp nor a lyre which the ladies-in-waiting played, and sometimes the minstrels who came to sing the news in ballads...»

No small part of the history of Castile, which was beginning to feel predominant, was forged within these walls of the castle of Arenas de San Pedro. The castle-palace also lived times of misadventure and was set alight by the French in 1809; the walls and turrets, however, remained proudly standing. The structure was partially rebuilt and some municipal offices have now been installed within the castle. But the castle's eternal occupant is perhaps the nostalgic feeling that Jorge Manrique expressed so superbly:

A view of Calle de Arenas de San Pedro.

El Aguila Caves.

That states and riches depart from us unexpectedly
Who doubts this?
We ask them not for permanence
For they are of a lady who moves on...
What became of King Don Juan?
The princes of Aragón,
What became of them?
What of all those courtiers?
What became of the ladies,
Their coiffures
Their dresses
Their scents?
What became of the flames
Of the fires fed by lovers?
What became of that troubadour,
The harmonious music
That played...?

Behind the walls of Arenas de San Pedro castle there only remain the memory of its radiant history and the Sad Countess's introspective grief. A stone witness to the glory of the capital of the «Andalusia of Avila», the old castle of the erstwhile Lord High Constable of Castile invites the visitor to pause and refine his sensitivity to facilitate the flight of historical evocation.
But it fell to the lot of the unfortunate Castilian lady of Arenas de San Pedro to have the honour of contributing decisively to the foundation of the monastery near the town, as the following document testifies:
«...And because I am very devoted to Our Lady the Holy Virgin María del Pilar, which is near to my "town of Arenas" and because the said monastery and its prior and friars and convent have my "charge to beg to God and to the said Our Lady the Holy Virgin Mary in their sacrifices and prayers for the soul of my master and lord", I hereby make over to them before God and for my lifetime and those of Count Don Juan and Doña María, my children, after our days... the bequest of six thousand maravedis from the rents of my town of Arenas. Executed in my town of San Martín de Valdeiglesias on the 12th of August, 1455. The "Sad Countess"».

The Castle of Don Alvaro de Luna, in Arenas de San Pedro.

The statue of San Pedro de Alcántara.

The tomb of San Pedro de Alcántara.

NUESTRA SEÑORA DEL CUBILLO AT ALDEAVIEJA

This shrine is about 4 kilometres from Aldeavieja. The church was built around 1460 to mark a miraculous event that happened there. The legend says that in the spring of 1454 a shepherd left a wooden pail with the tools that corresponded to his trade on one of the trees growing on the side of the hill. Suddenly, and without his being sure of the reason, he perceived something out of the ordinary: the presence of somebody and the presentiment that something supernatural was occurring around him. When he looked up at the tree where his pail was, he saw on top of it the ecstatic figure of the Virgin holding the Child. He fell to his knees and, clasping his hands together, contemplated the divine apparition. The Virgin spoke to the shepherd in a sweet voice and thanked him for the prayers he had dedicated to her and for the gifts he had offered up to her, encouraging him that a church in her honour should be raised up at that place. The apparition was repeated several times, even in the presence of other people.

It appears that the original hermitage of Nuestra Señora del Cubillo was small and composed of a single habitation, with a doorway in the main front and a bell gable on top. The present-day hermitage is an early Baroque church with a Latin cross ground-

The shrine of San Pedro de Alcántara.

Nuestra Señora del Cubillo *at Aldeavieja.*

plan and exterior in the Herrerian style. There is a vestibule beneath the choir and only one tower. The ceiling has groined barrel vaults and there is a spherical vault supported by pendentives in the transept.

The church is spacious but rather low, and the decoration is Baroque. In the interior one should note the high-altar dominated by the statue of the Virgin in the middle; the Virgin's magnificent niche dates from the 18th century and its pillars are decorated with bunches of grapes and vine leaves, coated with gold. You should also see three other Baroque altars; a window with an inscription and date, seemingly the year 1654; and another window, at the front, with a similar inscription and the date 1720 on its lintel.

By the hermitage there is an interesting building which was built in the 17th century, possibly to serve as an inn. One of the doors in the entrance hall on the ground floor leads to the church and another to the dining-room, a spacious habitation connected with two kitchens and two rooms serving as larders.

Taking a staircase from the entrance hall one may reach the first floor, where there is a central passageway with rooms on the left and right, two kitchens and two dining-rooms.

The *Virgen del Cubillo* is the patron saint of Aldeavieja and large numbers of worshippers, even from the provinces of Madrid, Segovia and Avila, visit the shrine. The exquisitely carved statue is very beautiful and has rich vestments and valuable jewels.

On Assumption Day the Virgin is dressed in a bright sky-blue mantle and, on the 8th of September, in a white mantle adorned with silver and gold and a silver crown with twelve stars, the points shining with precious stones. The silver half-moon displays several topazes.

A lovely close-up of Valdecorneja castle.

THE CASTLE OF VALDECORNEJA

The castle of Valdecorneja was built in the 14th century and, together with the ramparts of Barco de Avila, formed part of the river Tormes' system of defences. The castle, which has apparently borne its present name since Alfonso VI's time, dominates the river and the bridge. In olden days it had a double moat, stables and a portico with Romanesque arches; and was topped with Gothic crenellations. It was the home of the Lords of Valdecorneja and the Counts and Dukes of Alba. The rooms in which the duchess and her daughters lived faced west and gave on to splendid views, while the part occupied by the Duke and his sons faced the *Sierra de Gredos.* There was a further section of the castle, with a cistern and a hall with a high roof, given over to servants and to the soldiers who were garrisoned in the castle.

The chapel was in one of the towers and the ladies' boudoir in another. The main hall occupied a whole floor of the Homage Tower.

In the time of the *Reyes Católicos,* the parade ground was transformed into a courtyard for the guard of honour, enclosed within a gallery with Gothic battlements.

The castle was inhabited for some time by Don Fernando Alvarez de Toledo, Duke of Alba, Conqueror of Portugal and governor of the Netherlands. The mayor of the castle of Valdecorneja had orders not to surrender the castle «until breathing his last» or unless he heard the order from the very mouth of the Lord or King.

The river Tormes, Roman bridge and Valdecorneja castle.

BARCO DE AVILA

This historical town lies between the *Sierras* of Gredos and Béjar, on the right-land side of the river Tormes, at over 1,000 m. above sea-level. Barco de Avila is one of the most ancient towns in the province of Avila and draws its name from its strategic position which enabled it to control all movement on the river Tormes not far from its confluence with the river Aravalle.

During the Roman domination the early settlement acquired the status of *pagus,* or hamlet, and the Roman legions moving from Emérita Augusta to Avila had to pass through it. Their road was defended by *Torre del Cubo, Torre de Piedrahita, La Torre* and several other hilltop castles. Various Romanesque edifices were built at different times along this roadway, which was rebuilt after the Reconquest. The biggest arch was destroyed by the French during the War of Independence.

Barco de Avila still retains remnants of its ancient walls. Other very interesting monuments include the Roman bridge over the river Tormes, which was built in the 4th century; the Romanesque church inside which fine reredoses and screens are kept; several emblazoned mansions; and the hermitage of *El Cristo del Caño.*

Barco de Avila, which is situated near Gredos and the *Sierra de Solana,* is a place with great charm for tourists.

The town also offers the gastronomical incentive of the exquisite trout from the river Tormes.

◁ *Towers on the city wall.*
Churches of San Nicolás and Santa María.

Isabel la Católica's *room in the Augustin Convent.*

MADRIGAL DE LAS ALTAS TORRES

This is an historical town where Isabel I *la Católica* (the Catholic Queen) was born — in Juan II's palace, now restored — as were also Alonso de Madrigal *«El Tostado»* and the priest Vasco de Quiroga, magistrate of the Royal Court in Nueva España (now Mexico). Fray Luis de León, the great poet, died there in the old Augustin Monastery.
Another poet of considerable status, Miguel de Unamuno, dedicated this beautiful poem to Madrigal de las Altas Torres:

Ruins lost in a field
that was bed of the sea before of men,
your turrets bit the dust,
Madrigal de las Altas Torres.
You the cradle of Isabel, grave
of Don Juan, fateful origin;
he fell in gilded Salamanca
and in Avila, today funereal court
(...) Castile, Castile, Castile,
progenitor of upright men:
your castles bite the dust,
Madrigal of the High Towers,
ruins lost in the so soon dry bed
of an enormous marsh.

Madrigal is a town with a strong personality and still retains 23 of the 100 turrets which made up the old

The ancient Franciscan monastery at Cebreros.

ramparts, built in the 13th century or at the beginning of the 14th. Some of the gates, of fascinating architectural design, have also survived: the Moorish-influenced *Puerta de Peñaranda* is the most remarkable for its beauty and is also the best preserved. The ogival *Puerta de Cantalapiedra* and the *Medina* arch are extremely interesting, too.
The ramparts are built of mortar in the Mudejar style, with limestone and gravel between the bricks. The walls and towers of Madrigal are lower and not so thick on the east side. It seems that the walls and towers were painted white in olden days, which would be visually extraordinarily effective for the onlooker.

The finest of the high towers — which gave the town its name — is San Nicolás; an extensive view is to be had from it.
The most important monuments in Madrigal de las Altas torres include the church of San Nicolás which is a Romanesque-Mudejar monastery-cum-palace and inside which one should mention the Mudejar roof of the nave, the *Capilla Dorada* and the font where Isabel *la Católica* was baptised; the church of Santa María del Castillo where the fine Romanesque apses, with arches, are outstanding; and the *Convento de Nuestra Señora de Gracia,* which joins onto the 14th century palace where Doña Isabel was born. The square and the old hospital are also interesting.

CEBREROS

The courts of the district are in this town, which is about 800 m. above sea-level. It is 43 km. from the capital of the province, half-way between El Tiemblo and El Hoyo, and near the *Puerto de Arrebatacapas.* Cebreros is surrounded by the vineyards which produce the esteemed *«albillo»* grapes. The wine from the Cebreros area, which is dense and very alcoholic, is justly famous and very appropriate for drinking with roasts, or any other meat dish.

The most important monuments are the splendid parish church and the atmospheric ruins of the 15th century Franciscan Monastery. The place called *Picota de Piedra* is also interesting.

From Cebreros one can make a charming excursion to the majestic *Salto del Alberche* waterfall.

Overall view of Cebreros.

Overall view of Arévalo.

AREVALO

This is an historic town situated on top of a hill. It was repopulated in 1088, after the Reconquest, and Enrique IV held court there. The Prince of Viana was born, and Doña Juana «the Mad» died, in Arévalo. It was at one time one of the key strategical points in Castile's defences. Unamuno writes: «Arévalo basks in the sun of Castile, and raises the towers of its churches and monasteries to the sky in the tongue of land formed by the confluence of the rivers Adaja and Arevalillo.

It resembles a promontory, with picturesque escarpments to the rivers, and the ruins of the old castle stand on the very extreme of this tongue, at such a height that they look down on the courses of the two rivers and on the two bridges. A massive old tower that speaks of old rancours and the times when the nationality was laboriously forged».

The old castle has an octagonal ground-plan and is famous for the important rôle it played at the time of the Reconquest; the impressive Homage Tower is outstanding. The most remarkable of the other monuments in Arévalo are the remains of the walls; the church of Saint Martin, which has a handsome Romanesque portico and fine Mudejar towers; the church of Santa María, where there is a Mudejar apse with arcades along the wall; San Miguel church; San Nicolás church, with a beautiful façade raised in the early 17th century; the churches of Santo Domingo and San Juan de los Reyes; and the diverse ancestral mansions and stately homes that the visitor will discover in the course of a stroll through the town.

An imposing shot of the historical castle of Arévalo.

A magnificent close-up of the Plaza de la Villa.

FONTIVEROS

This township, at an altitude of 886 m above sea-level, lies in the judicial district of Arévalo and is the capital of La Moraña Alta. Fontiveros played an outstanding part during the Middle Ages. Alphonso 'the Warlike' of Aragon and his troops killed Blasco Jiménez and his nephew Lope Núñez near its walls. A monument called Cruz del Reto ('Cross of the Challenge') was raised to commemorate this occurrence, and survives to this day.

S John of the Cross, the great mystic poet, was born in Fontiveros in 1542. A small church was built at the house where he was born, contiguous to the Carmelites' convent. The image of this Saint is attributed to Gregorio Fernández.

The most remarkable monuments in the town are San Cipriano church, in the Gothic/Mudejar style, with a fine panelled ceiling; the Ayuntamiento (Town Hall), surmounted by artistic decoration; and several houses with escutcheons on their façades. The Mudejar style is predominant in some buildings.

San Cipriano church: high altar reredos.

Monument to S John of the Cross.

Overall view of Candeleda.

CANDELEDA

A picturesque village at the feet of the *Sierra de Gredos.* The prehistoric cloister and necropolis at the *Collado de Freilillo,* and the *Monasterio de Nuestra Señora de Chilla* are very interesting. The houses, typical of this mountain region, have the wooden structural part on the outside. The Rosarito reservoir, on the river Tiétar, is situated very near Candeleda.

Sanctuary of Nuestra Señora de Chilla.

The famous Bulls of Guisando.

THE BULLS OF GUISANDO

The famous Bulls of Guisando are to be found in a meadow four kilometres away from San Martín de Valdeiglesias. These are four bulls sculptured in granite, and their origins are Iberian.

The 14th century Monastery of Guisando stands very near this location, there the Castilian nobles swore to overthrow Enrique IV and proclaim Doña Isabel *la Católica* queen.

San Martín de Valdeiglesias is a very ancient town and conserves numerous interesting monuments such as the castle, with its lofty Homage Tower, the ruins of the Bernadine Friars' abbey, the 11th century Romanesque bridge over the river Alberche, the unfinished church built by Juan de Herrera and the hermitage of *La Nueva,* inside which a small Byzantine sculpture of the Virgin is kept.

There is also a very interesting and artistic corner balcony dating from the 16th century which gives on to the *Calle Mayor.*

San Martín de Valdeiglesias is also famous for the magnificent bullfights that take place there on the occasion of the town's *fiestas* in the first fortnight of September.

El Tiemblo, with a beautiful 16th century church, is situated ten kilometres away from the celebrated Bulls of Guisando. Around El Tiemblo, the Alberche reservoir has abundant fishing and magnificent sporting and hotel facilities at the disposition of visitors. Because of all this, the area has become an important centre of tourism.

Overall view of the castle at Navas del Marqués.

NAVAS DEL MARQUES

A sizable summer resort in the *Sierra de Malagón,* surrounded by beautiful pinewoods, at 1,219 m. above sea-level. The name of the village derives from «Navas», that given to the flat lands located between mountains distributed for settlements by Don Ramón of Burgundy at the time of the repopulation of the Avila area. The feudal estate of Las Navas was granted to the Count of Santisteban, first Marquis of Las Navas and third Count of Risco. The Marquisate dates from the time of Carlos V.

The important monument in Navas del Marqués is the old castle which is built on a sturdy and well-founded granite rock.

The Homage Tower still survives from the original castle, which apparently dates from the 11th century.

A legend connected with the castle relates that an extraordinarily beautiful maiden named Magalia, the daughter of a feudal lord who lived in the fortress, fell in love with a centaur, no less; the girl fled from the castle one night, mounted on the back of her mythical lover.

Other interesting monuments in Navas del Marqués are the 15th century parish church and the ruins of the Monastery.

The landscapes surrounding the village are of great beauty; this, together with the healthy climate, has converted the place into an important centre of tourism. The *«Ciudad Ducal»,* a magnificent residential area with excellent hotel and sporting facilities, is not far from the village.

A charming view of the castle at Mombeltrán.

MOMBELTRAN

A picturesque village situated in the *Sierra de Gredos,* near Arenas de San Pedro. The landscapes around Mombeltrán are powerfully attractive due to their fascinating and unusual beauty.

The village has a fine 15th century Gothic parish church with, inside, superb reredoses and screens; also the interesting ruins of the *Convento de Santa Rosa,* and the Hospital, which is a noteworthy 16th century building.

But the most important monument in Mombeltrán is the Dukes of Alburquerque's castle: it dates from the 16th century.

This famous castle is connected historically with the personage of Don Beltrán de la Cueva, Count of Ledesma, Duke of Alburquerque and master of the Order of Santiago, who was, it seems, the lover of Doña Juana de Portugal, Enrique IV's wife. Fruit of Doña Juana's affair with the Duke of Alburquerque, a daughter was apparently born, she went down in history with the nickname Juana *«la Beltraneja»* and was recognised as heiress to the throne of Castile by the *Cortes* (the Parliament) in 1465.

Against the wishes of the Archbishop of Toledo and a large number of noblemen, Enrique IV decided to annul the disposition of the *Cortes* and named his brother Alfonso as heir. Enrique IV nonetheless rectified his position soon after, and the noblemen gathered in Avila formally dethroned him. The nobles

Town hall, Mombeltrán.

who were opposed to *«la Beltraneja»* inheriting the crown of Castile were undecided for a period after the death of the *Infante* Don Alfonso and espoused the cause of Isabel *la Católica,* whom Enrique IV finally recognised as his successor in the meadow where the Bulls of Guisando stand.

Mombeltrán castle asserts its harmonious architectural outline on the top of a hill which looks down on a vast and beautiful view threaded by the valley of the river Tiétar.

The castle is reached through a gate with a semicircular arch topped with the coat of arms and ducal crown of Alburquerque. The fortress had a deep moat and a drawbridge; and its defences were reinforced by embrasures which surrounded the castle.

Inside, the parade ground remains, ringed by a wall with battlements. Access to the interior is through an inside door protected by machicolations crowned with towers, these display checkered coats of arms with stars or hearts.

The sections of the castle used by the lords made up an ensemble of three floors. It also contained dungeons and wine-cellars in the lower levels.

The Homage Tower and the capitals on the central columns of the lower gallery are profusely adorned with granite coats of arms: eagles, lions, stars, hearts and other motifs, all artistically carved.

When Don Beltrán de la Cueva's wife embraced her husband at the castle door she exclaimed «Mon Beltrán!» and this is the name the village bears today.

Contents

Text, photographs, lay-out, design and printing by EDITORIAL ESCUDO DE ORO, S.A.

11th Edition - I.S.B.N. 84-378-0530-9 Dep. Legal. B. 14804-1998